The art of climbing in windows

:

There are no pebbles large enough to awake sleepers in sleep.

You cannot stumble down hallways through shafts of light

So brilliant, As offered up to the day on a platter of thought.

You come in the night with your head in your lap,

Rapping on windows and putting out porch lights.

She leans her head out and you say,

" Come down, and I will show you a magic place."

But it is long past the hour of dreams, all that is now, Is black.

You cannot just bust through the windows of Love like a

Sunbeam, LIKE-IT-Or-Not.

There is an art to climbing in.

You do it in dark Places and ask Blue Why Violet never showed up.

You find your way In On the Wails Of a Saxaphone.

You close The shutters to Make Sure desire does not see,

You Play your games and Leave Quietly,

Going back the way you came.

And In the Morrow You Find your way down other streets,

Where Other Windows Await.

out of the blue

There is A body in the sky

And faces hangin everywhere

Full of uncertain contemplation

and upside down Frowns.

And it feels like I'm standing still

while you move madly around me

So what keeps me from moving?

What holds me in place with feet like concrete?

It was your letter that made me smile,

It was your laughter that made me cry,

It was the gift you gave that made me dance,

And it was what you said that made me think.

"COME BACK!" I cried. You choked on those last few words,

And I could bearly make out what you said.

And if I could move fast enough, I'd catch up to you,

Just to tell you that you left the most important thing behind...

Me....

THE LOW-BOYS part 1: RISE

I Picture A MoMenT in All Of ThiS WheRe The MuNdane MoVes OveR,

BreAkiNG THesE Mad WaVes ARoUnd me And Peeling back the layers... An OVerLappiNg

of Well SeemiNg Forms Struck Down By AnGels In The AtMosPheRe...

ReVealiNg Lifes LoW-BoYs, LiNear MOtionS and The defiNitioN OF all HoPe LOSt....

A Place BeLOw the Surface WherE The broken Toys Go Down ScrEamiNg, SpiTTing

FlamEs and ShattEring StaiNed gLass. A VisiON of The HAY DyiNG in the Fields,

A DeafiniNg SilieNCe thAt surrounds All Of uS. The DeepEst of Dark ReaChing oUt

to ReTrieve Us at RandoM... The ABYss UnfoLding itseLf In The Light Of

DARK DAYS DAWniNG... The VieW Up ThRough The BottoM....

Dry LeaVes TuRniNG To AshEs, DISEnTIGRATION!!!

Fractured And Beautiful

I'm Not sleeping much.
The weather inside has got me down.
I tried to meet the moon out back but I missed it.
So now I am prying it from my lovers eyes,
So we can give it back to the night as if it were something we never depended on.
With it caught in her gaze she is Blinding,
Fragmented and Beautiful.
We are not making room for another in these palaces so private.
I like it quiet in these halls so she can tiptoe around the tourments.
The paintings here are like windows into worlds we will never wander.
Maybe if these walls were deeper I could move out past them and lay your diamonds where they belong.
But it seems I have always been here on the edges of dawn.
Covering these lands
with curtains and shaking the shadows from the lampstands.
Taking on formlessness so I can find her in every room.
This is no home for heroes.
There will be no peace in here tonight.
These have become the rooms that only chaos can build.
A new addition with each passing day.
We have made our homes on broken avenues;
And with the doors locked and the moon in our eyes....
We Are Happy.

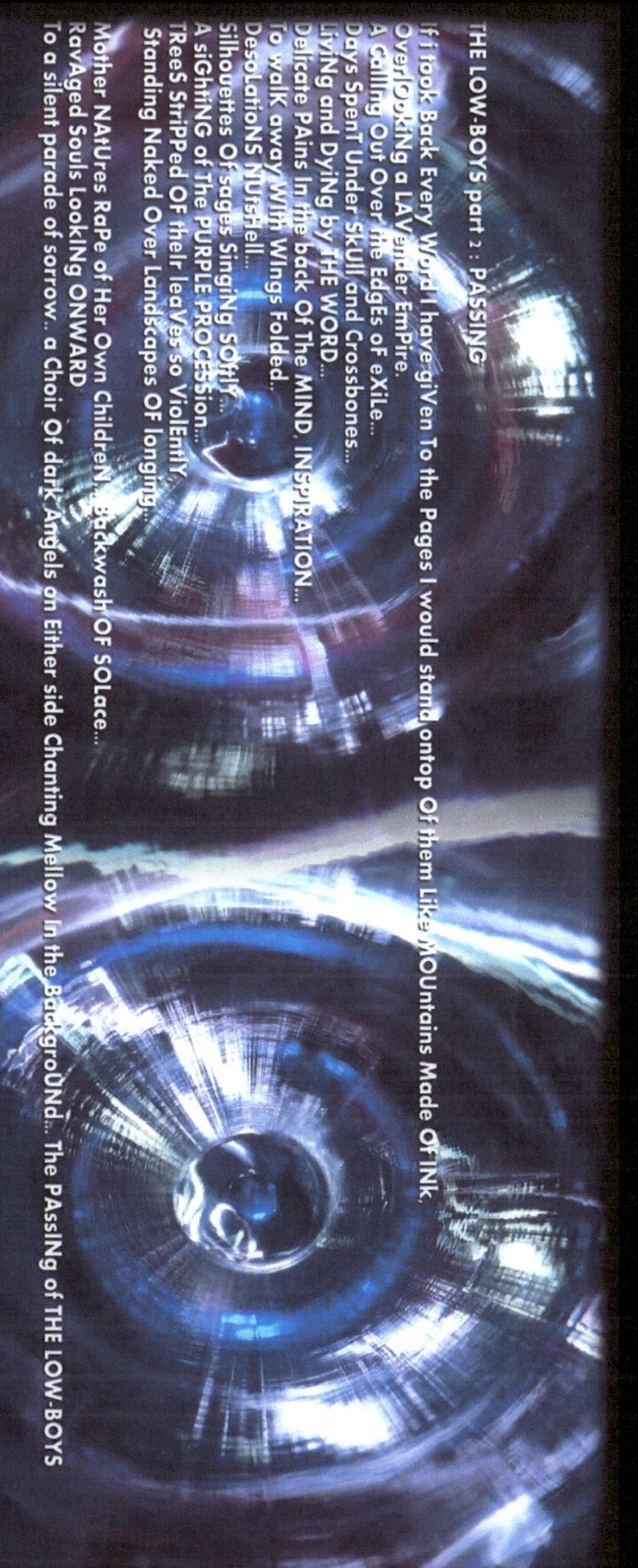

THE LOW-BOYS part 2 : PASSING

If i took Back Every WorD I have giVen To the Pages I would stand ontop Of them Like MOUntains Made Of INk.
OverlOoKiNg a LAVender EmPire.
A calliNg Out Over the EdgEs of eXile...
Days SpenT Under sKUll and Crossbones...
LiviNg and DyiNg by tHE WORD.
Delicate PAins in the back Of The MIND. INSPIRATION...
To walK away WiTh Wings Folded.
DesoLatioNS NUrsHell...
silhouettes Of sages SingiNg sOngs...
A siGhiNG of The PURPLE PROCeSSion...
TReeS StriPPed Of their leaVes so ViolEntly
Standing Naked Over LandScapes Of longing...

MOther NAtUres RaPe of Her Own ChildreN. BackwasH OF SOLace...
RavAged Souls LooKiNg ONWARD
To a silent parade of sorrow... a Choir Of darK Angels on Either side ChantiNg Mellow In the BackgroUNd... The PAssINg of THE LOW-BOYS

The Sharpening of my Tongue

I don't want to be plucked from the shadows,
Or pulled in close by high priced pricks or buzz cut bitches.

I want to taste death from the end of a PEN,
I want the clouds to pass through me instead of around.
I need the afternoon sun with occasional greys
So it doesn't always go down blonde,
And chase my eyes between dark glass and tear.

I need a hand to hold onto when it all rattles round
crazy like, in my mind.

A sweet voice calling me out into midnight madness.

What then my dreams would become
What evident treasures these are.

And I will not hang my head in sadness
To acknowledge each melancollie moment without you
As my own.

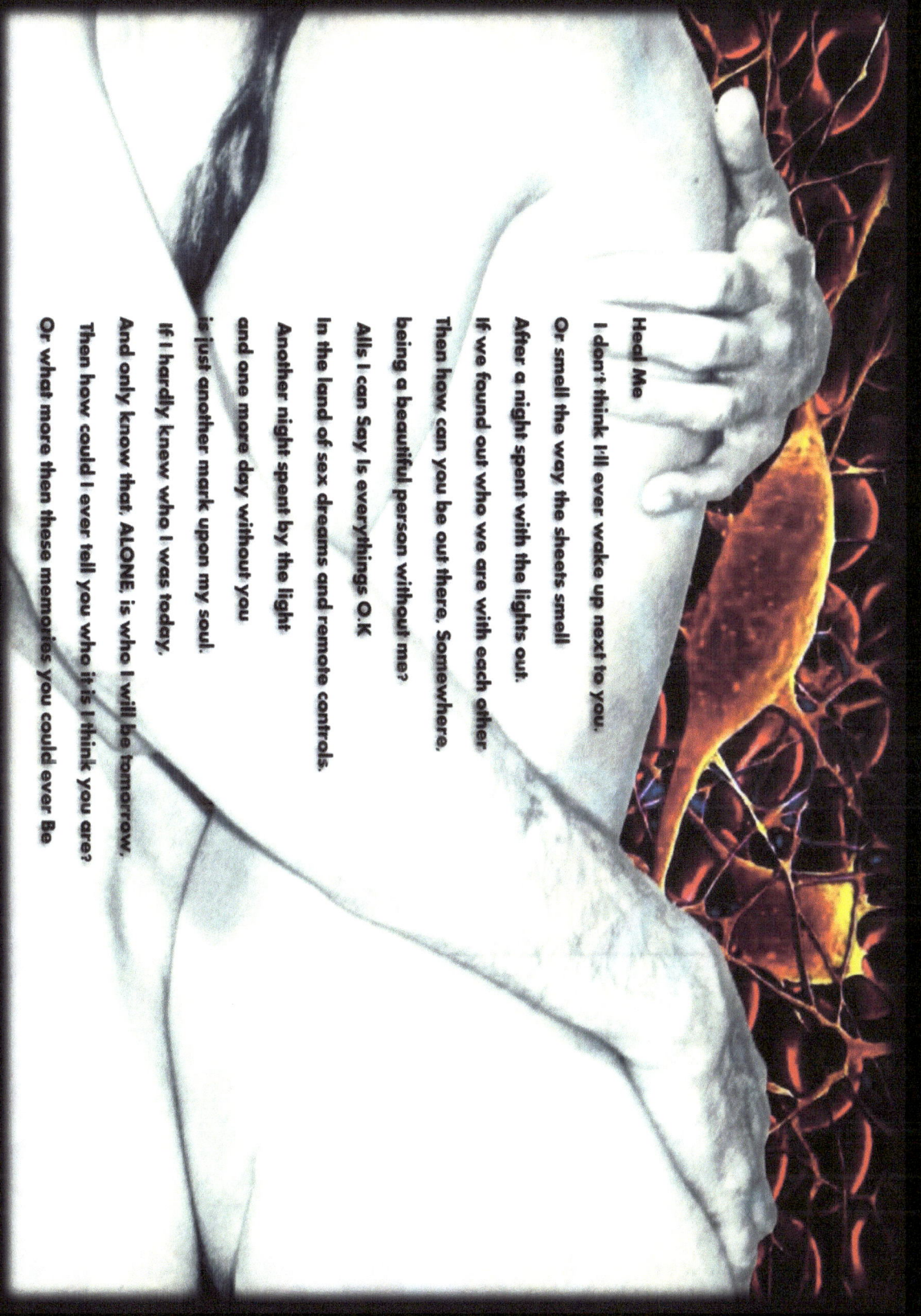

Heal Me

I don't think I'll ever wake up next to you.

Or smell the way the sheets smell

After a night spent with the lights out.

If we found out who we are with each other

Then how can you be out there. Somewhere.

being a beautiful person without me?

Alls I can Say Is everythings O.K

In the land of sex dreams and remote controls.

Another night spent by the light

and one more day without you

is just another mark upon my soul.

If I hardly knew who I was today.

And only know that, ALONE. is who I will be tomorrow.

Then how could I ever tell you who it is I think you are?

Or what more then these memories you could ever Be

In the Turning

The wool forever stays tight over your eyes,

Believing you are better now,

but still skinny sick on the inside.

Pretending there were never wounds there,

Your wearing someone elses life.

You traded your old one in,

Hoping no one would remember what it looked like.

Putting it on a shelf for some other fool to find,

feeling renewed with some balancing act.

There are wild flowers to be picked,

Somewhere there are arches to walk through,

You have covered up your curiosities,

and are busy drowning out the memory.

Browsing rejuvenation,

Remaining convinced and certain,

You never owned those faces,

They were only borrowed,

YOu took a tour of something that

was too deep for you to understand.

Leaving the reflections coverd,

You want to believe you are changing,

that you were seen there on the cliffs in summer.

You were letting go of effigies and

burning pictures of lives two sizes too big,

Crying out over monoliths,

saying someday, we're gonna get right with the world.

Give me a quiet moment away from this delicate disaster at sea.
High tide is beyond being breakers and I am Crashing.
Spreading out over these miniature wars I'm fighting on the inside,
This battlefield is RAGING!!!
We are reaching out in waves we never wanted
Searching for secrets behind the pictures,
I tossed a handful of pins to see what would happen
and it was beautiful and amazing.
Silent soft explosions and my world spread out past their
straight and narrow.
I collected a handful of sentences to bring back across the borders.
Found inspiration in this ear piercing pain and gave it a name.
I have served in the armies of the FALLEn
and waded through words to get here.
Standing on the shores of this illusion
I can see the ghosts of lighthouses and they are calling us home.
but its a dangerous raod to recover, these pins are everywhere
We couldnt hold them when they were together
and now we cant see them when they are apart.
and i am spitting stones while no one is looking.
Your in the canyons living in glass towers.

My pages are frozen, stuck in these surroundings and seperated.
I want to look at this world with my eyes closed and listen
for the trumpets when their blown.
Once I wanted to believe that there was something more
then this all the while looking over my most.
Someday I might take a break from this breakdown
But for now it is my sea.
And one by one I will give you these pins
hoping you'll make them into something
more beautiful then lighthouse ghosts and veils of night.
See because I am on the edges of a town called BECOMING.
And though I have never been I know that I am welcome there.
I will tell the tale of tossing pins into the ocean with YOu.
I will lay these words in the spaces that fall between us.
ANd I'll Look Up into the canyons, And Know that YOu are there.

veRSE bY TraVis whitE
PHOtogRaphY bY DaVid CaRTwriGht
www.facebook.com/miniaturethoughtsideasandblackouts
http://www.flickr.com/people/miniaturethoughtsideasandblackouts

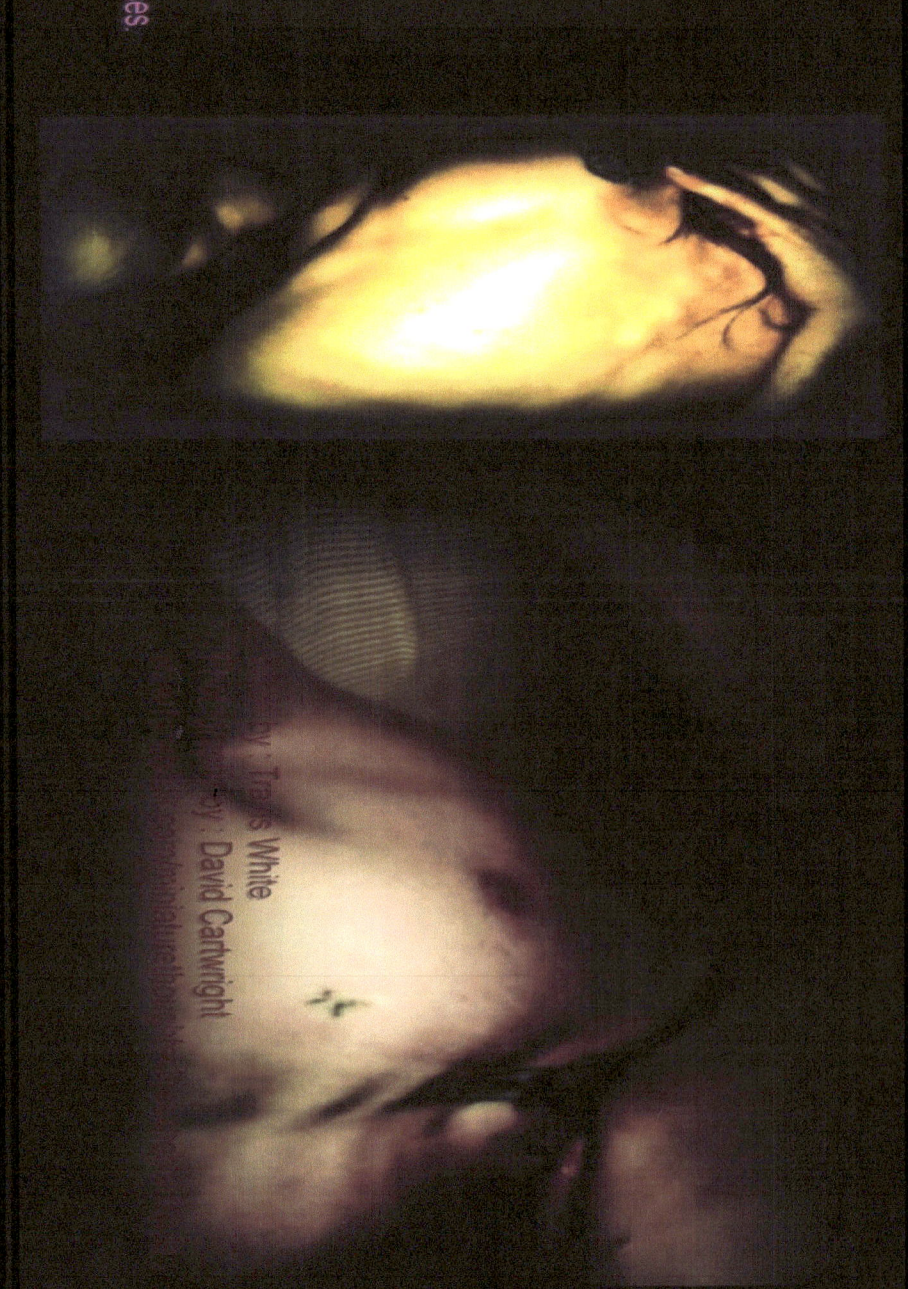

COMMITMENT

I am not afraid anymore
I am tracing the steps that
Brought me to this point
And crowning them.
The commitment.

The time between now and then
Is cracked and registers
With the pain of silent children.

A cloud is summoned in a
Horrible second of uncertainty.
I was doubled on the skylines
Poisoned by the possibilities
Of the Hollow-Pointed mind.
I am the offspring of these phantom phases.
A vapor that passes through you.
And overseer to the secrets of our night.

Poem by: Travis White

Photography by: David Cartwright

eprived. Alive

And left dead standing.

One night in trade

for an eternity between the sheets.
Give me lust in place of luXury.

A challenge behind
the red eyes of a kiss.

verse by: TraVis WhiTe.
PhotogRaphy bY: DaVID CarTwrGht.
www.facebook.com/miniaturethoughtsideasandblackouts
http://www.flickr.com/people/miniaturethoughtsideasandblackouts

PASTS PRESENT

Looking outside these windows to a place where
the past is just a sad little face.
We give life with the most honest of intention.
Weeding through these stone gardens.
Watching our little light grow over them
and become the master of its own shadow.
We stay aimlessly awake and drifting.
Crossed out and crooked.
We've come to an age where we run a wire through everything.
Trying to lean on what remains unseen.
There is no simple path preceeding
the roads we walk will lead us back to where we started.
If it were that easy to see past all this dark
we would have flipped the switch years ago.
I would have washed my hands of all of this
and maybe even came home to you.
But I am rooted so high upon this hill
I have even seen your sadness come and go.

Passing through me like mist in mourning
only to leave me soaked and sorry to the soul.
I threw a wrecking ball in your direction
and you caught it and carried it back.
Swinging iron fists and screaming out at me
" Keep YOur World Of WreckAge!!
You seem to Wear It Oh so Well."

verSe bY: TraVis WhiTe
PhOtoGraphY bY: DaVid CaRTwRIGht
www.facebook.com/miniaturethoughtsideasandblackouts
http://www.flickr.com/people/miniaturethoughtsideasandblackouts/

Ghost Dance

Formlessly they pass before us. Translucent armies of movements
Rhythmic transformations into waves and wave forms.
Spaces between us and voices echoing across time.
Caught in a celebration of souls I watch them and I am amazed.
I can see them. Coming into focus now.
These movements are known as ghost dancing
and these long hours I dedicate to the taming of the muse are now mine.
Mine to hold and mine to keep.

VeRse By: TRaVis WhiTE
phOtoGraphY by: DaVid CamunCilT

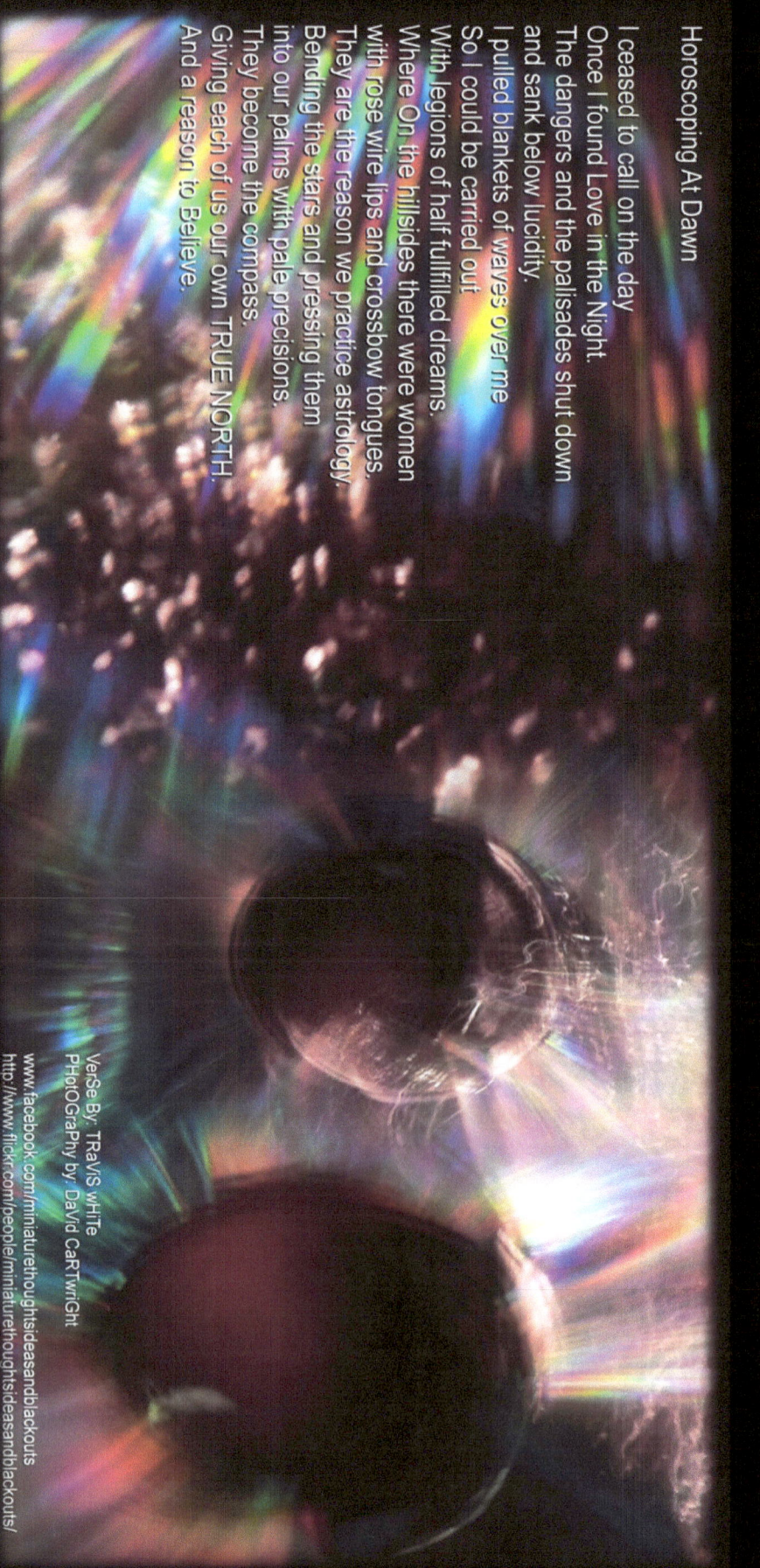

Horoscoping At Dawn

I ceased to call on the day
Once I found Love in the Night.
The dangers and the palisades shut down
and sank below lucidity.
I pulled blankets of waves over me
So I could be carried out
With legions of half fulfilled dreams.
Where On the hillsides there were women
with rose wire lips and crossbow tongues.
They are the reason we practice astrology.
Bending the stars and pressing them
into our palms with pale precisions.
They become the compass,
Giving each of us our own TRUE NORTH.
And a reason to Believe.

VerSe By: TRaViS wHiTe
PHotOGraPhy by: DaViD CaRTwriGht
www.facebook.com/miniaturethoughtsideasandblackouts
http://www.flickr.com/people/miniaturethoughtsideasandblackouts/

Grey Be Gone

From day to day the mind splits
in two different directions.
One choosing the side of Desire,
The other ducking out the back with common sense.
Feeling the need for things that are instant,
and quick to bow down in services of the flesh.
Straddling fences watching to see which side
shines in brighter color.
Waiting out indecision.
Saying its been decided,
Molding perceptions like clay figurines
with invisible hands.
Enfolded, the heart is weakening to surrender.
Battle lines, Sides chosen,
It leaves the body in sieges of collapse.
Splintering on impact.
Ripples and images after THE FALL.
Anxious shivers of various Black.
Unheard Ever spinning.
Becoming faint and distant.
Drifting Away~

Truth in Transformation

It would seem I am no longer young.
Outside the eyes of infantcy
I recieved the painful wisdom.
wanting to become drowned in languages
I slipped in to the recesses
between the earth and sky.
There was music when I serviced
my eyes to Nods.
Heatwaves and Harmony.

A thin angel came to me in the mornings
Revealing the vanity I lost with my purity.
This became a beacon in the confusion.
An awkward circle that is never ending.

VerSe bY TraViS wHiTe
PhoTogRaphY By: DaVid CartwRIGht
www.facebook.com/miniaturethoughtsideasandblackouts
http://www.flickr.com/people/miniaturethoughtsideasandblackouts/

caught you staring at the backs of mirrors.
Celebrating ceremonies and lines in the dirt.
We are Under the Auroras now, Hypnotized and Spun.
Pointing at fractals of the forest You are lost.
An evil wind is blowing from behind the mountains,
And i can see in color now,
the way we were before.
You said you were planning a Rebirth,
shedding this life for another,
like scales and skin.
And to meet you there before the masses.
In a different light looking back on whats BROKEN and BLUE.
And I have wore these masks in hopes of changing.
have given all I have and more.
We will buy new lives in the Narrows next week,
and wear them on sidewalks of Uncertainty.
We will feel loved.
as if we have never been before.

Where the center *will not hold*

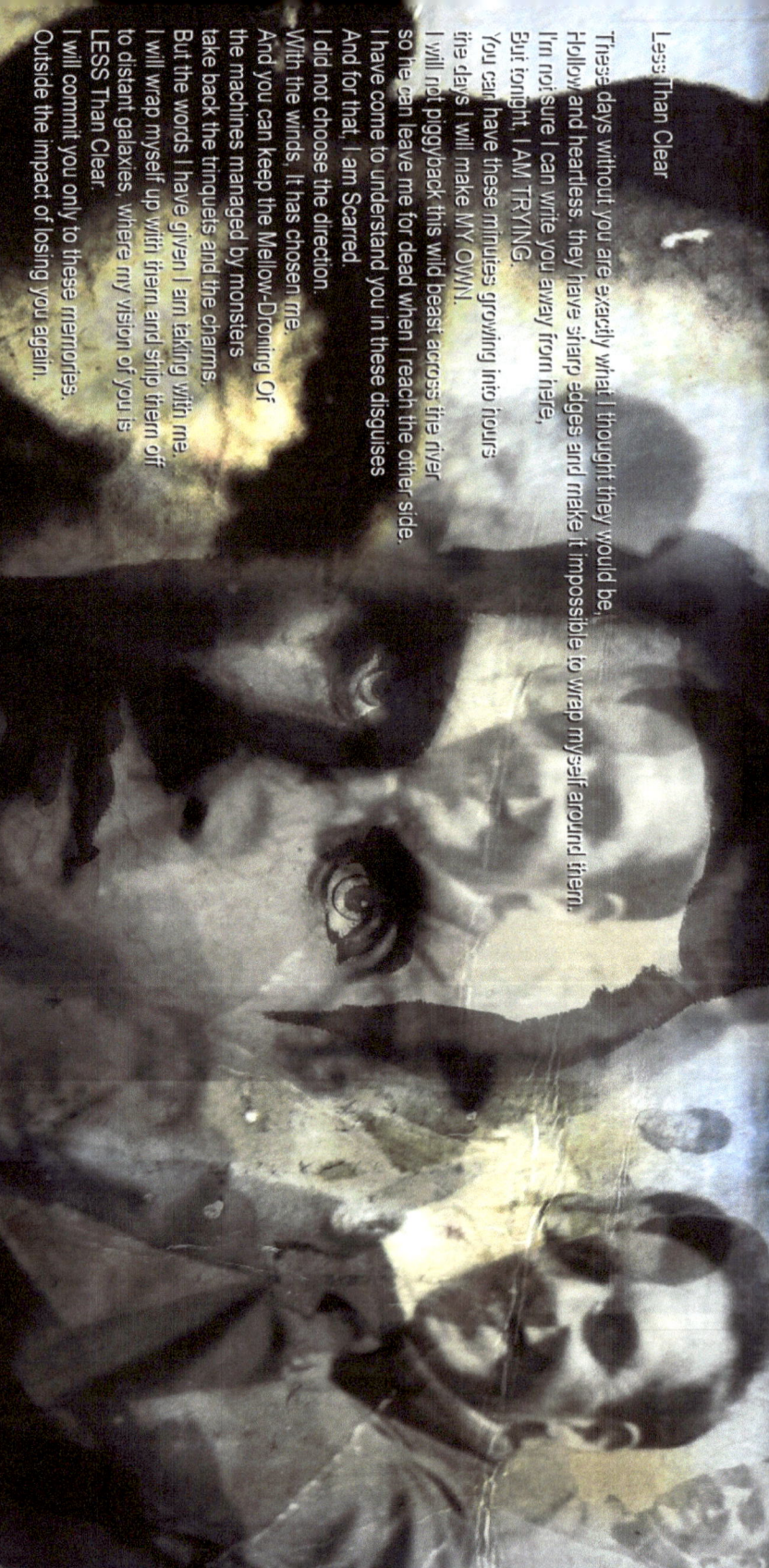

Less;Than Clear

These days without you are exactly what I thought they would be,
Hollow and heartless, they have sharp edges and make it impossible to wrap myself around them.
I'm not sure I can write you away from here,
But tonight, I AM TRYING.
You can have these minutes growing into hours
the days I will make MY OWN.
I will not piggyback this wild beast across the river
so he can leave me for dead when I reach the other side.
I have come to understand you in these disguises
And for that, I am Scared.
I did not choose the direction.
With the winds, it has chosen me.
And you can keep the Mellow-Droning Of
the machines managed by monsters
take back the trinquets and the charms.
But the words I have given I am taking with me.
I will wrap myself up with them and ship them off
to distant galaxies, where my vision of you is
LESS Than Clear.
I will commit you only to these memories.
Outside the impact of losing you again.

VeRse bY: TrAVis wHITE
photography by: DaVid B. CartWriGht

Glass Walking On Someday Street

This is the street you dream about in your sleep
Where sometimes the distances are greater
Then the distances from Bed to Bed
Where in the rain we here are
And all things seemingly possible
I rolled over in divisions of SOMEDAY StrEEt
Where there are dragons in the windows of the churches
and cracked bells that ring out in rhythm
There is a lady three stories closer to heaven
that will break bottles at your feet
as you side-step the sidewalks
Saying she is fresh out of rose pedals
Broken glass shall be the path
The lucidity of languages and lampposts
Hold us upright to the ungrieved
No one here wears the crown
This is no paradise but it will suffice
A suspended city where Violent Violins
Come crying form the cobblestones
Red limning the gauges and picking the pockets of destiny.

We bend into what seems Looming and Majestic
So far above it all now the rooftops come up to meet our feet
And it is the end of my wanderings
I will go back there SOMEDAY
I will stare on the first floor and work my way to heaven
I may choose to lay the path or just go Glass walking
Laughing In a space where time cannot touch us
And Old faces are Happiest When it rains

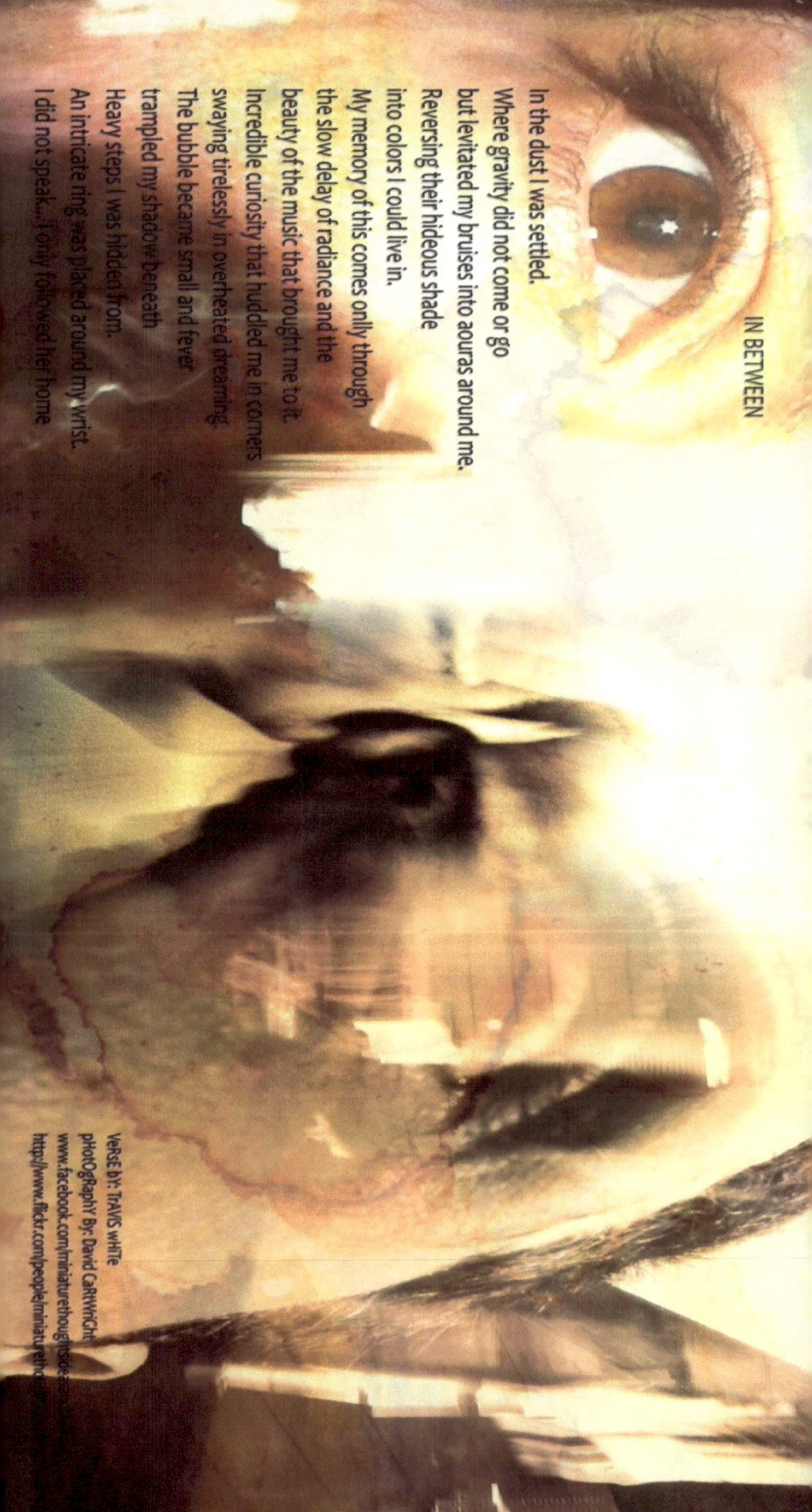

IN BETWEEN

In the dust I was settled.
Where gravity did not come or go
but levitated my bruises into auras around me.
Reversing their hideous shade
into colors I could live in.
My memory of this comes only through
the slow delay of radiance and the
beauty of the music that brought me to it.
Incredible curiosity that huddled me in corners
swaying tirelessly in overheated dreaming.
The bubble became small and fever
trampled my shadow beneath
Heavy steps I was hidden from.
An intricate ring was placed around my wrist.
I did not speak...I only followed her home

VeRSE bУ: TRAVIS wHiTe
pHotOgRaphУ BУ: David CaRwinCht
www.facebook.com/miniaturethoughtsideas
http://www.flickr.com/people/miniaturetho

THE LOW-BOYS part 3: FALL

The LesseR Of Two Evils.....

The GreatEr Of The Gods....

ApOllO is GatheriNg his ChilDren In The BackYard FoR a SmOke out....

And The StReets Are FillEd With SilEnt parades...

PoPPy Fields On the HoRiZon....

FroM MomenTs To MillEstones....

raPTuRe To RhapSodY....

TherE are Giants Out there LuRKINg TeariNg down MOUNtains With GiaNT ToNes...

And For ONce It dosent seem so bad to Have Been passed over By Giant Eyes....

Big Hands HoLdinG us From The HERE-AFTEr-NOW....

BeiNG kepT wide AwakE By The hearraChe... Out of touch and Overcome.. ReCkOnINg!!!

Deep EyEs DrAwIng The StormS.... LiNes In The sAnd FroM The Dragging Of Crosses...

FaiNt RemInderS Of whAt We Left beHind...OnE By onE... SinkINg Back BelOw the SufAce...

THEY FALL.

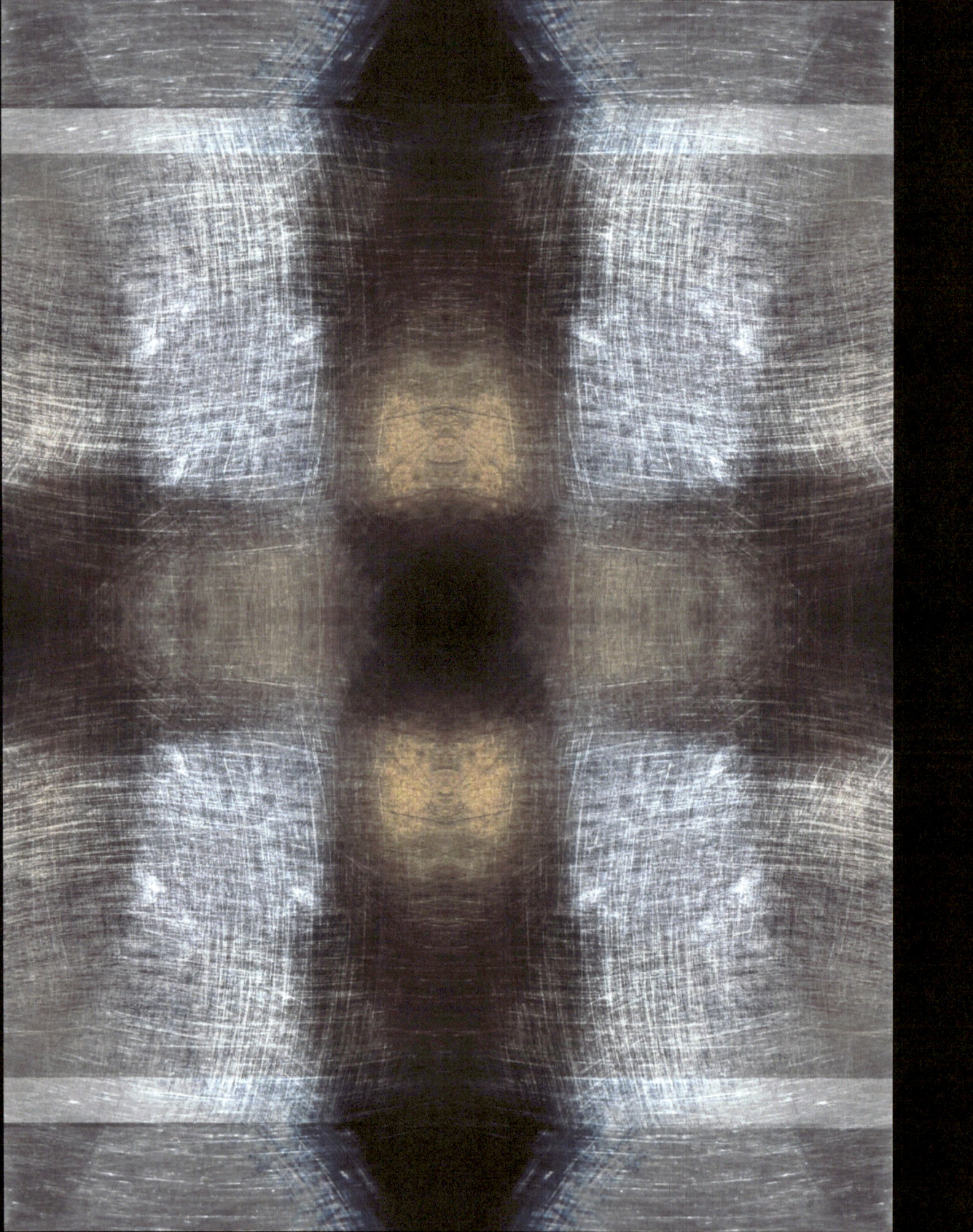

The Author:

Travis White

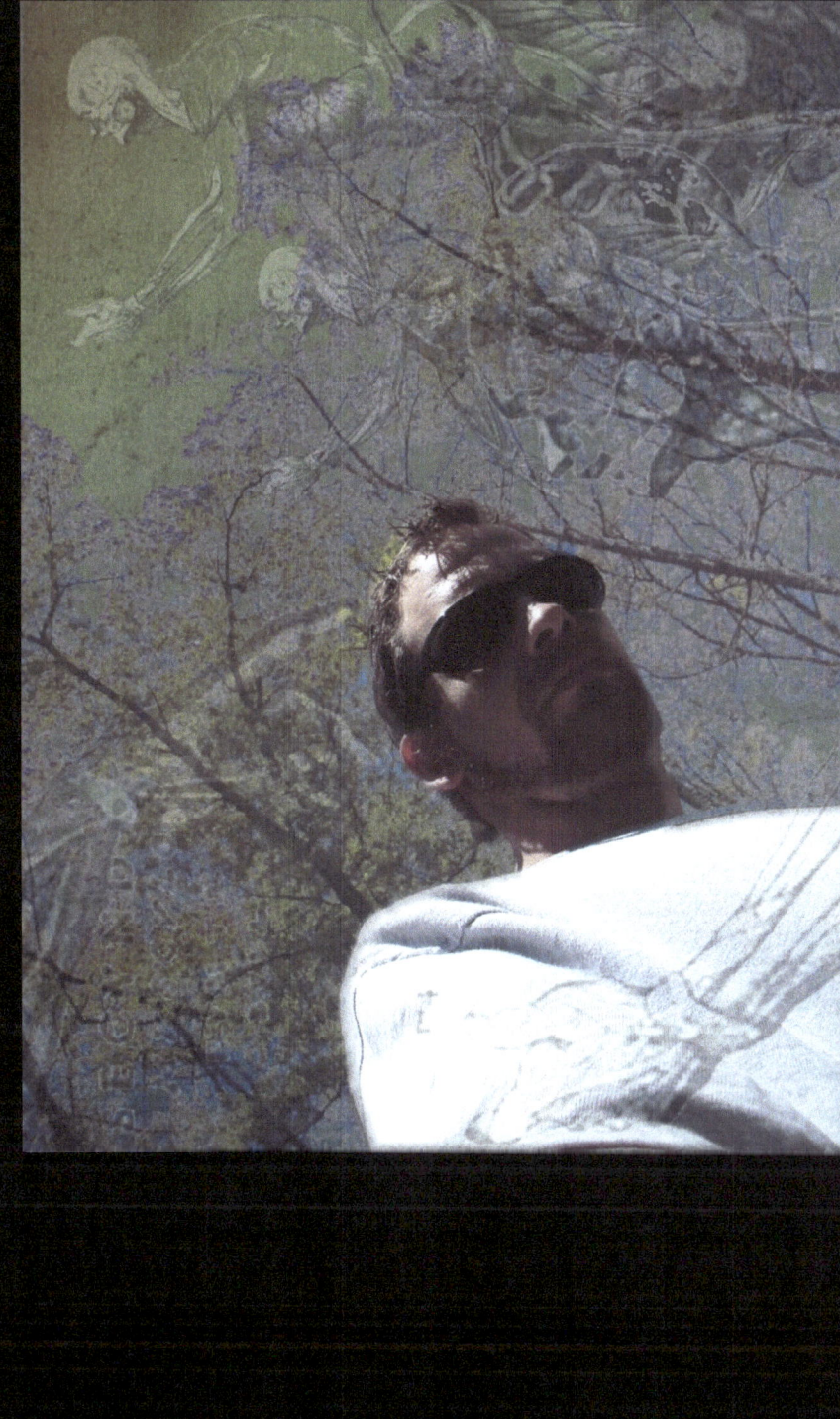

My Yawn is a silent scream to the world.

A shout out-over-and beyond.....

... Calling all stars,

Be on the lookout for one hopeless dreamer.

Known to hangout in nights skies,

Long, low afternoons,

And sometimes shady places.

Last seen wearing h his soul on his sleeve,

His heart in his pocket, and his head in a bag.

He's known to let loose lonely,

and hide it all behind warm words

and crooked smiles.

Guide him SAFE, SOMEWHERE, DISTANT.

And with your eyes,

See him somewhere soft enough

to cushion two peoples landing.

Because when he falls down to you,

He doesn't want to land ALONE.

Travis White

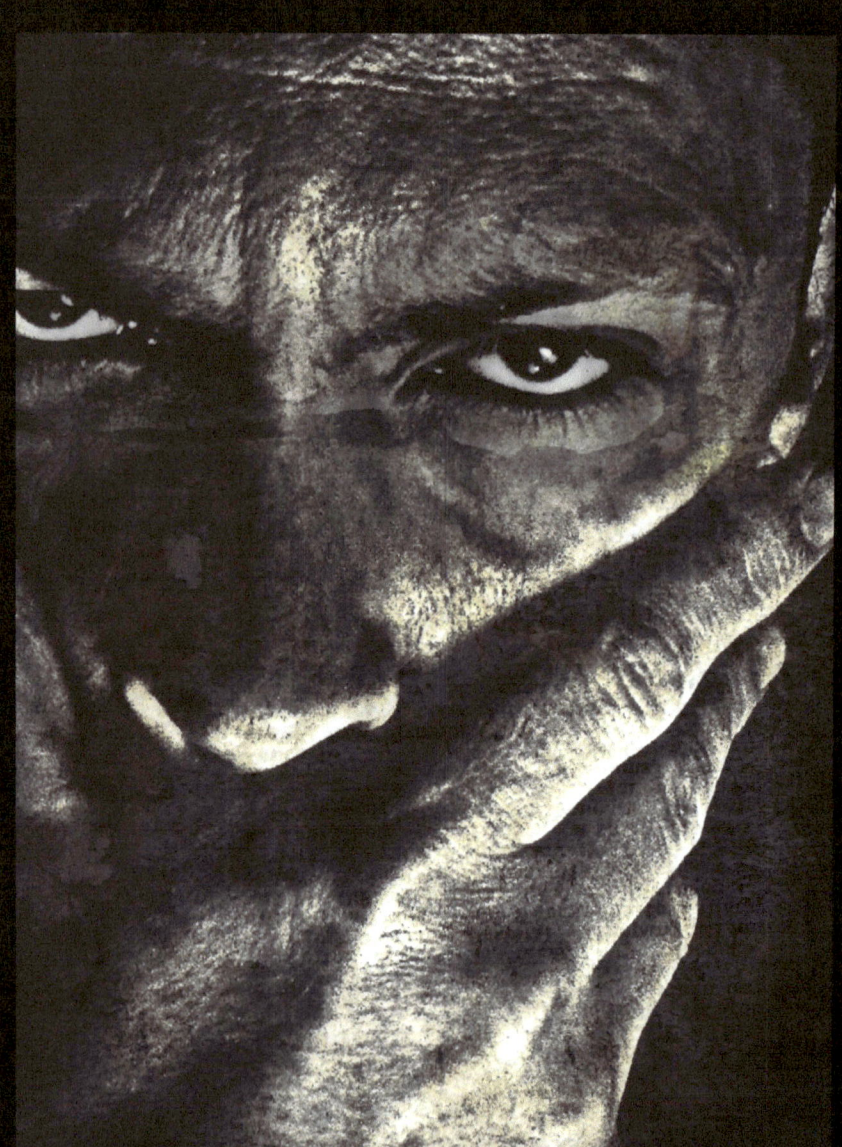

http://www.flickr.com/photos/miniaturet
houghtsideasandblackouts/

 The Photographer(?):

David Cartwright

www.ingramcontent.com/pod-product-compliance
Lightning Source LLC
Chambersburg PA
CBHW050913180526
45159CB00007B/2893